SELECTIONS FROM

ABBA®

GOLD

GREATEST HITS

HAL•LEONARD®

Published by
Hal Leonard

Exclusive Distributors:
Hal Leonard
7777 West Bluemound Road,
Milwaukee, WI 53213
Email: info@halleonard.com

Hal Leonard Europe Limited
42 Wigmore Street,
Marylebone, London WIU 2RY
Email: info@halleonardeurope.com

Hal Leonard Australia Pty. Ltd.
4 Lentara Court, Cheltenham,
Victoria 9132, Australia
Email: info@halleonard.com.au

Order No. AM1004432
ISBN: 978-1-78038-436-8
This book © Copyright 2011 by Hal Leonard

Edited by Adrian Hopkins.
Cover designed by Liz Barrand.

All Songs: Vocals: Aileen McLaughlin & Jules Dodd
Chiquitita
Dancing Queen
Mamma Mia
Money, Money, Money
Waterloo
The Winner Takes It All
arranged and performed by Paul Honey
All other songs:
Guitars: Arthur Dick.
Bass: Don Richardson.
Drums: Chris Baron.
Keyboards: Paul Honey.
Arranged by Paul Honey.
CD recorded, mixed and mastered by Jonas Persson.

Printed in the EU.

www.halleonard.com

Chiquitita
(Andersson/Ulvaeus) Bocu Music Limited/Bocu (ABBA) Music

Dancing Queen
(Andersson/Anderson/Ulvaeus) Bocu Music Limited/Bocu (ABBA) Music

Fernando
(Andersson/Anderson/Ulvaeus) Bocu Music Limited/Bocu (ABBA) Music

I Have A Dream
(Andersson/Ulvaeus) Bocu Music Limited/Bocu (ABBA) Music

Knowing Me, Knowing You
(Andersson/Anderson/Ulvaeus) Bocu Music Limited/Bocu (ABBA) Music

Mamma Mia
(Andersson/Anderson/Ulvaeus) Bocu Music Limited/Bocu (ABBA) Music

Money, Money, Money
(Andersson/Ulvaeus) Bocu Music Limited/Bocu (ABBA) Music

The Name Of The Game
(Andersson/Anderson/Ulvaeus) Bocu Music Limited/Bocu (ABBA) Music

S.O.S.
(Andersson/Anderson/Ulvaeus) Bocu Music Limited/Bocu (ABBA) Music

Super Trouper
(Andersson/Ulvaeus) Bocu Music Limited/Bocu (ABBA) Music

Take A Chance On Me
(Andersson/Ulvaeus) Bocu Music Limited/Bocu (ABBA) Music

Thank You For The Music
(Andersson/Ulvaeus) Bocu Music Limited/Bocu (ABBA) Music

Voulez-Vous
(Andersson/Ulvaeus) Bocu Music Limited/Bocu (ABBA) Music

Waterloo
(Andersson/Anderson/Ulvaeus) Bocu Music Limited/Bocu (ABBA) Music

The Winner Takes It All
(Andersson/Ulvaeus) Bocu Music Limited/Bocu (ABBA) Music

Chiquitita

WORDS & MUSIC BY BENNY ANDERSSON & BJÖRN ULVAEUS

A **Asus⁴** **1.** **A** **Asus⁴** **2,3.** **A**

| / | / | / / | / | / | / | :| / | / | / | / |

sad, so qui - et.   2. Chi-qui-ti - ta, tell me the   Chi-qui-ti - ta, you and I
up to - geth - er.)
sad, so qui - et.)

D

| / | / | / | / | **5/4** / | / | / | / | / |

know,   how the heart - aches come and they go and the

A   **E**   **D**

| **4/4** / | / | / / | / | / | / | / | / | / / | /

scars they're leav- ing.   You'll be danc-ing once a-gain   and the pain will

E   **A**

| / | / | / | / | / | / | / | / |

end,   you will have   no   time for griev- ing.

          D

| / / | / | / | / / / | **5/4** / | / | / | / |

Chi-qui-ti- ta, you and I cry   but the sun is still in the sky and

A

| **4/4** / | / | / | / | / | / | / | / |

shin - ing a - bove you,   let me hear you sing once

E   **D**   **E**   **A**

| / | / | / / | / | / | / / | / | / | / / | /

more like you did be-fore, sing a new song, Chi-qui-ti - ta.

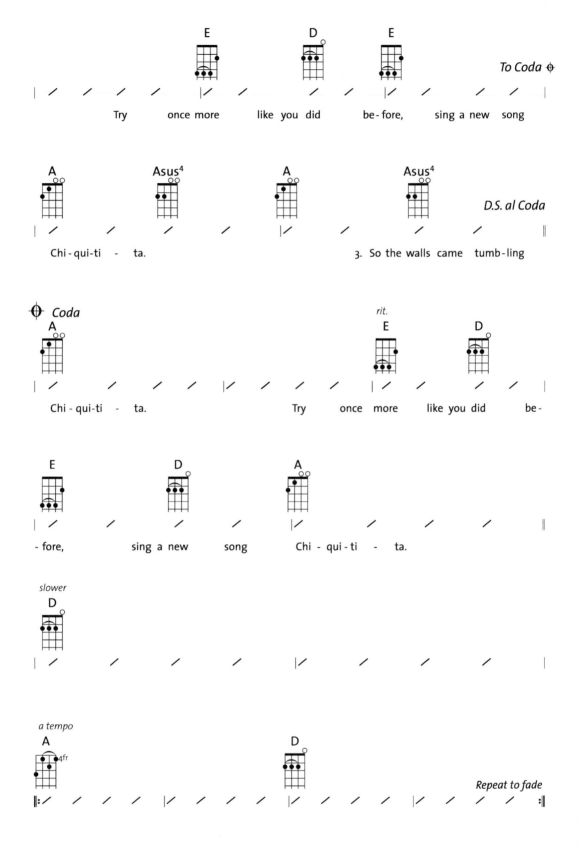

Dancing Queen

Words & Music by Benny Andersson, Stig Anderson & Björn Ulvaeus

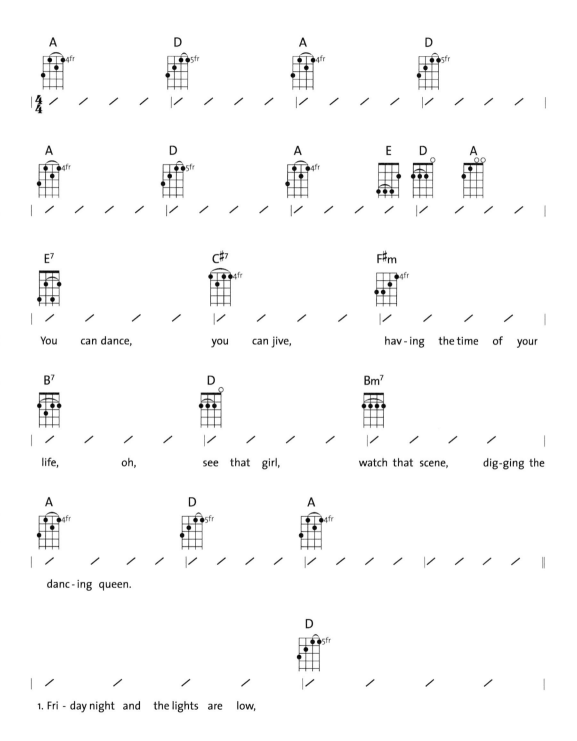

You can dance, you can jive, hav-ing the time of your

life, oh, see that girl, watch that scene, dig-ging the

danc-ing queen.

1. Fri-day night and the lights are low,

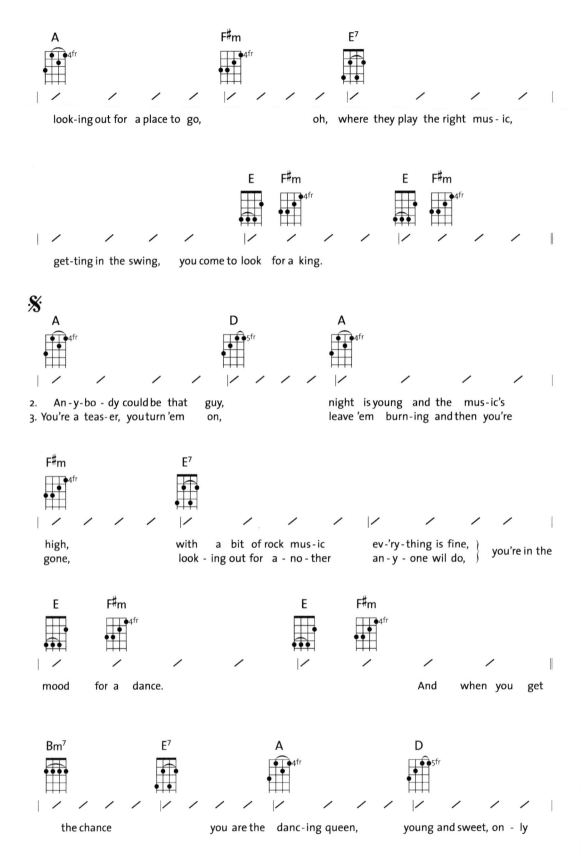

A   F#m   E7

look-ing out for a place to go,   oh, where they play the right mus-ic,

E   F#m   E   F#m

get-ting in the swing,   you come to look for a king.

𝄋

A   D   A

2. An-y-bo - dy could be that   guy,   night is young and the   mus-ic's
3. You're a teas-er, you turn 'em   on,   leave 'em burn-ing and then you're

F#m   E7

high,   with a bit of rock mus-ic   ev-'ry-thing is fine, ⎫
gone,   look - ing out for a - no-ther   an-y - one wil do, ⎬ you're in the

E   F#m   E   F#m

mood   for a   dance.   And   when you get

Bm7   E7   A   D

the chance   you are the danc-ing queen,   young and sweet, on - ly

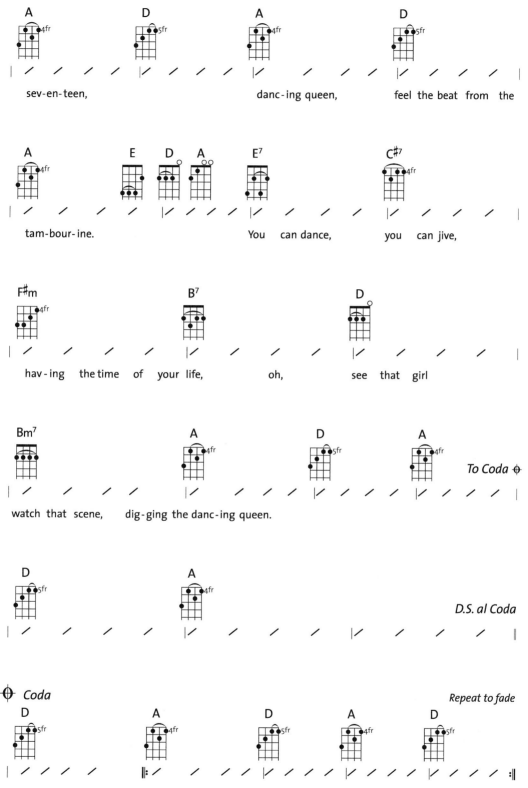

sev-en-teen,   danc-ing queen,   feel the beat from the

tam-bour-ine.   You can dance,   you can jive,

hav-ing the time of your life,   oh,   see that girl

To Coda

watch that scene,   dig-ging the danc-ing queen.

D.S. al Coda

Coda   *Repeat to fade*

Dig-ging the dan-cing queen.

9

I Have A Dream

WORDS & MUSIC BY BENNY ANDERSSON & BJÖRN ULVAEUS

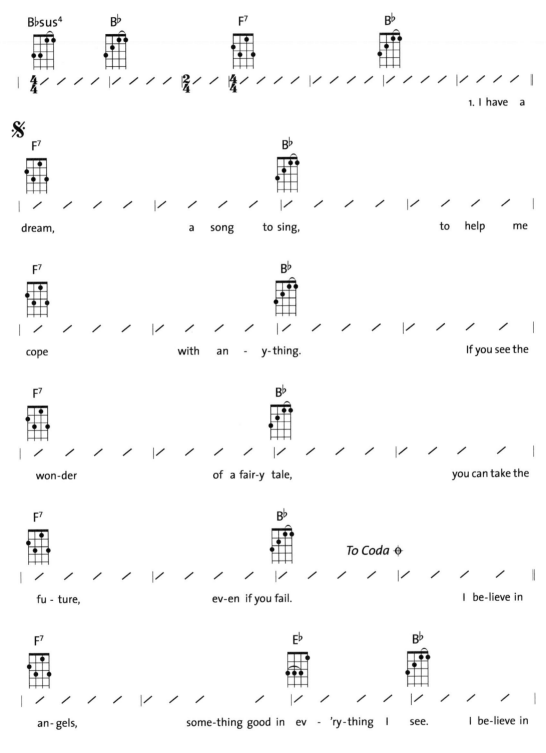

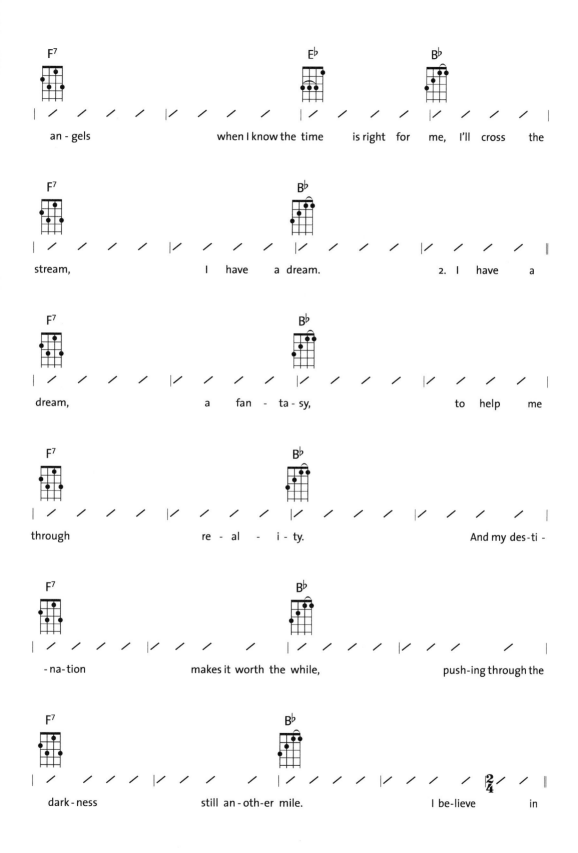

F⁷   E♭   B♭

an - gels   when I know the time   is right for   me,   I'll   cross   the

F⁷   B♭

stream,   I   have   a   dream.   2.   I   have   a

F⁷   B♭

dream,   a   fan - ta - sy,   to   help   me

F⁷   B♭

through   re - al - i - ty.   And my des-ti -

F⁷   B♭

- na-tion   makes it worth the while,   push-ing through the

F⁷   B♭

dark - ness   still an - oth-er mile.   I be-lieve   in

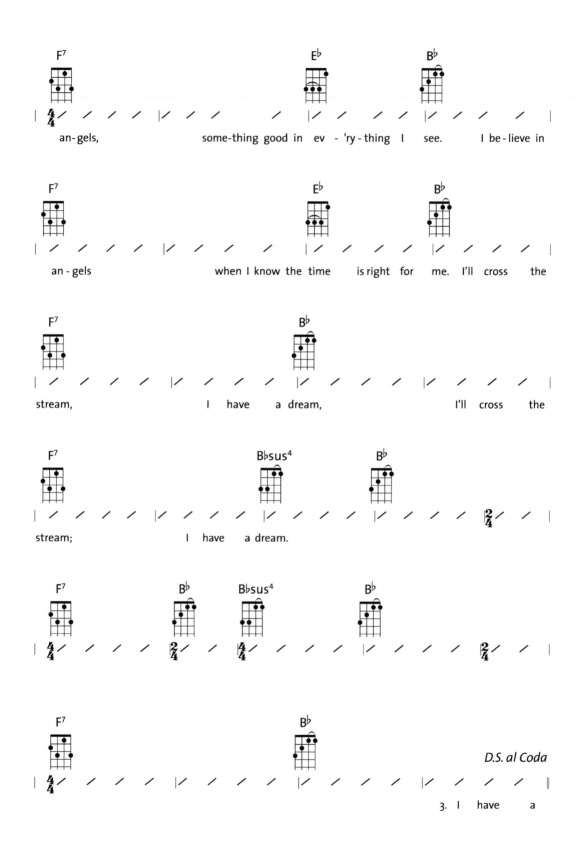

F⁷   Eᵇ   Bᵇ

| **4/4** / / / / | / / / / | / / / / | / / / / |

an- gels,   some-thing good in ev - 'ry-thing I   see.   I be - lieve in

F⁷   Eᵇ   Bᵇ

| / / / / / | / / / / | / / / / | / / / / |

an - gels   when I know the time   is right for   me. I'll   cross   the

F⁷   Bᵇ

| / / / / / | / / / / | / / / / | / / / / |

stream,   I   have   a dream,   I'll   cross   the

F⁷   Bᵇsus⁴   Bᵇ

| / / / / / | / / / / | / / / / | / / / / **2/4** / / |

stream;   I   have   a dream.

F⁷   Bᵇ   Bᵇsus⁴   Bᵇ

| **4/4** / / / / **2/4** / / **4/4** / / / / | / / / / **2/4** / / |

F⁷   Bᵇ

D.S. al Coda

| **4/4** / / / / | / / / / | / / / / | / / / / ‖

3. I   have   a

12

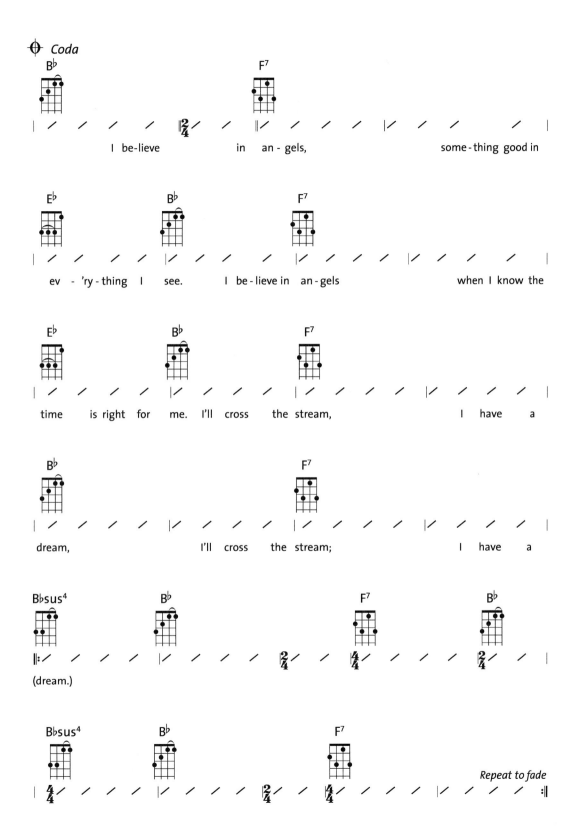

⊕ *Coda*

I be-lieve in an-gels, some-thing good in ev-'ry-thing I see. I be-lieve in an-gels when I know the time is right for me. I'll cross the stream, I have a dream, I'll cross the stream; I have a (dream.)

Repeat to fade

Fernando

WORDS & MUSIC BY BENNY ANDERSSON, BJÖRN ULVAEUS & STIG ANDERSON

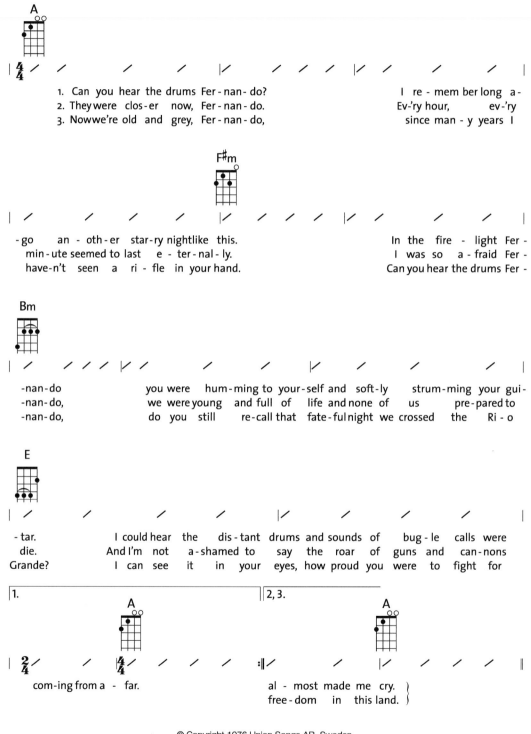

A

1. Can you hear the drums Fer - nan - do?   I re - mem ber long a-
2. They were clos - er now, Fer - nan - do.   Ev-'ry hour,   ev-'ry
3. Now we're old and grey, Fer - nan - do,   since man - y years I

F#m

- go   an - oth - er star-ry night like this.   In the fire - light Fer -
min - ute seemed to last   e - ter - nal - ly.   I was so a - fraid Fer -
have-n't seen a ri - fle in your hand.   Can you hear the drums Fer -

Bm

-nan-do   you were   hum-ming to your-self and soft-ly   strum-ming your gui-
-nan-do,   we were young   and full of   life and none of   us   pre-pared to
-nan-do,   do you still   re-call that   fate-ful night we crossed   the   Ri - o

E

- tar.   I could hear   the   dis-tant drums and sounds of   bug-le   calls were
die.   And I'm not   a-shamed to   say   the roar   of   guns and   can-nons
Grande?   I can see   it   in   your   eyes, how proud you   were   to   fight for

1.

A

com-ing from a - far.

2, 3.

A

al - most made me cry.)
free-dom   in   this land.)

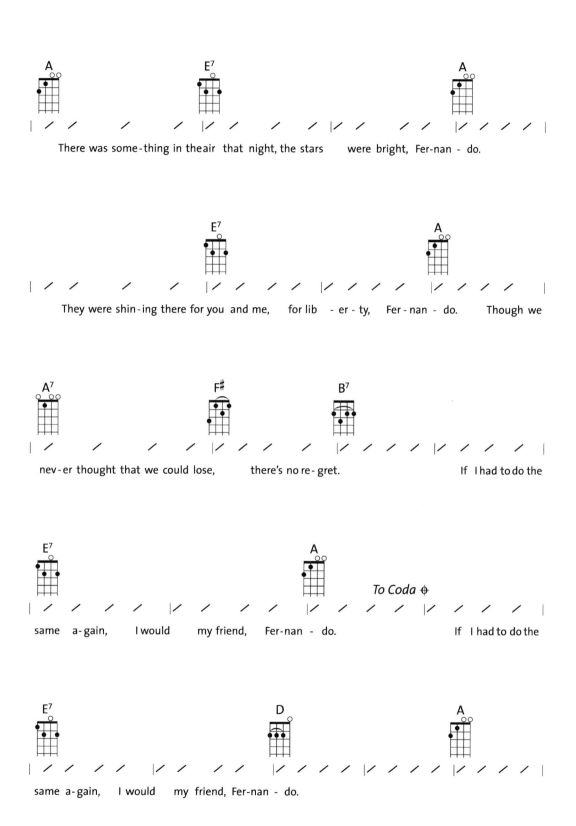

There was some-thing in the air that night, the stars were bright, Fer-nan - do.

They were shin-ing there for you and me, for lib - er - ty, Fer - nan - do. Though we

nev - er thought that we could lose, there's no re - gret. If I had to do the

To Coda ⊕

same a-gain, I would my friend, Fer-nan - do. If I had to do the

same a-gain, I would my friend, Fer-nan - do.

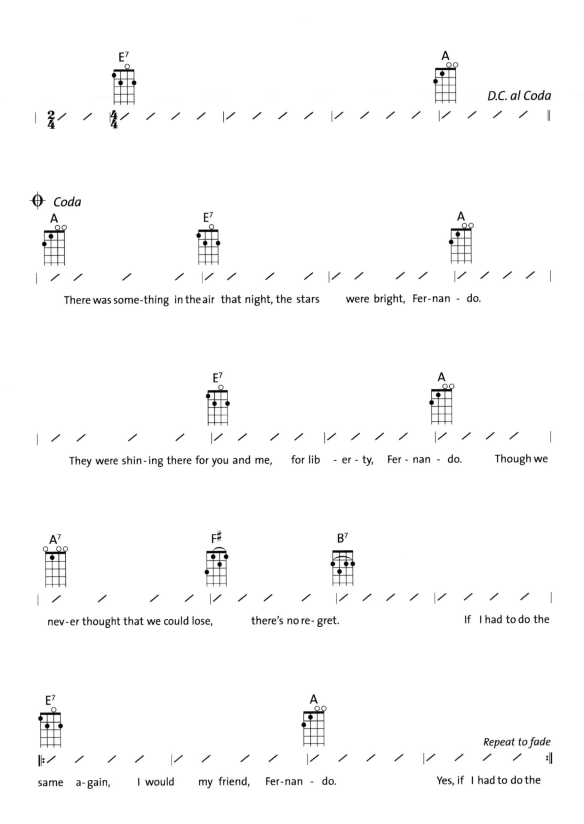

$\left|\begin{array}{c}2\\4\end{array}\right|$ ╱ $\left|\begin{array}{c}4\\4\end{array}\right|$ ╱ ╱ ╱ | ╱ ╱ ╱ ╱ | ╱ ╱ ╱ ╱ | ╱ ╱ ╱ ╱ ‖

D.C. al Coda

Coda

| ╱ ╱ ╱ ╱ | ╱ ╱ ╱ ╱ | ╱ ╱ ╱ ╱ | ╱ ╱ ╱ ╱ |

There was some-thing in the air that night, the stars   were bright, Fer-nan - do.

| ╱ ╱ ╱ ╱ | ╱ ╱ ╱ ╱ | ╱ ╱ ╱ ╱ | ╱ ╱ ╱ ╱ |

They were shin-ing there for you and me,   for lib - er - ty, Fer - nan - do.   Though we

| ╱ ╱ ╱ ╱ | ╱ ╱ ╱ ╱ | ╱ ╱ ╱ ╱ | ╱ ╱ ╱ ╱ |

nev-er thought that we could lose,   there's no re- gret.   If I had to do the

Repeat to fade

‖: ╱ ╱ ╱ ╱ | ╱ ╱ ╱ ╱ | ╱ ╱ ╱ ╱ | ╱ ╱ ╱ ╱ :‖

same a- gain, I would my friend, Fer-nan - do.   Yes, if I had to do the

16

Mamma Mia

WORDS & MUSIC BY BENNY ANDERSSON, STIG ANDERSON & BJÖRN ULVAEUS

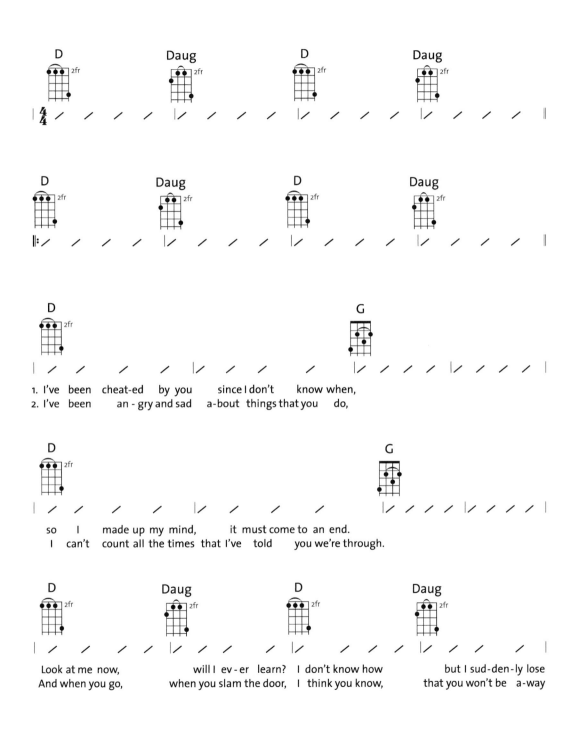

1. I've been cheat-ed by you   since I don't   know when,
2. I've been   an - gry and sad   a-bout things that you   do,

so   I   made up my mind,   it must come to an end.
I   can't   count all the times that I've   told   you we're through.

Look at me now,   will I ev - er   learn? I don't know how
And when you go,   when you slam the door, I   think you know,

but I sud-den-ly lose
that you won't be   a-way

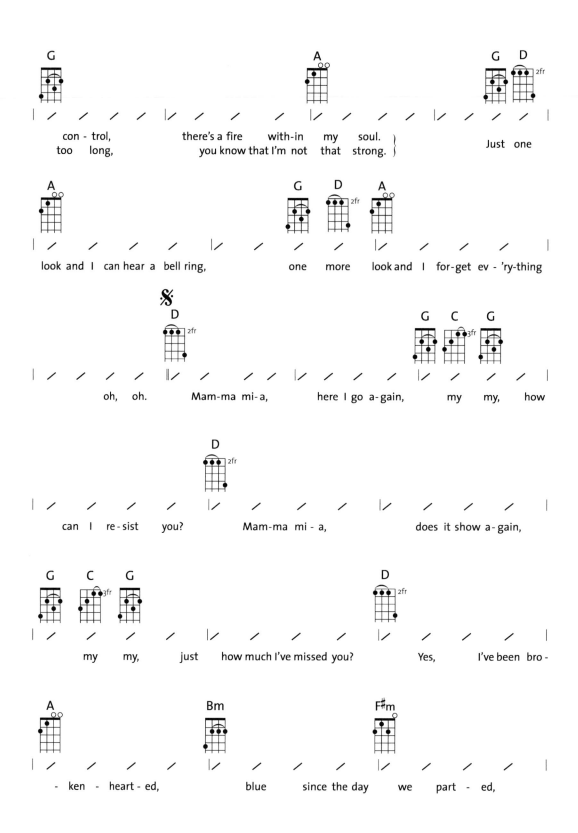

G   A   G   D

con - trol,   there's a fire   with-in   my   soul. ⎫
too   long,   you know that I'm not   that   strong. ⎭   Just   one

A   G   D   A

look and I can hear a bell ring,   one   more   look and I   for-get ev - 'ry-thing

𝄋
D   G   C   G

oh,   oh.   Mam-ma mi- a,   here I go a-gain,   my   my,   how

D

can I re-sist   you?   Mam-ma mi - a,   does it show a-gain,

G   C   G   D

my   my,   just   how much I've missed you?   Yes,   I've been bro -

A   Bm   F#m

- ken - heart - ed,   blue   since the day   we   part - ed,

18

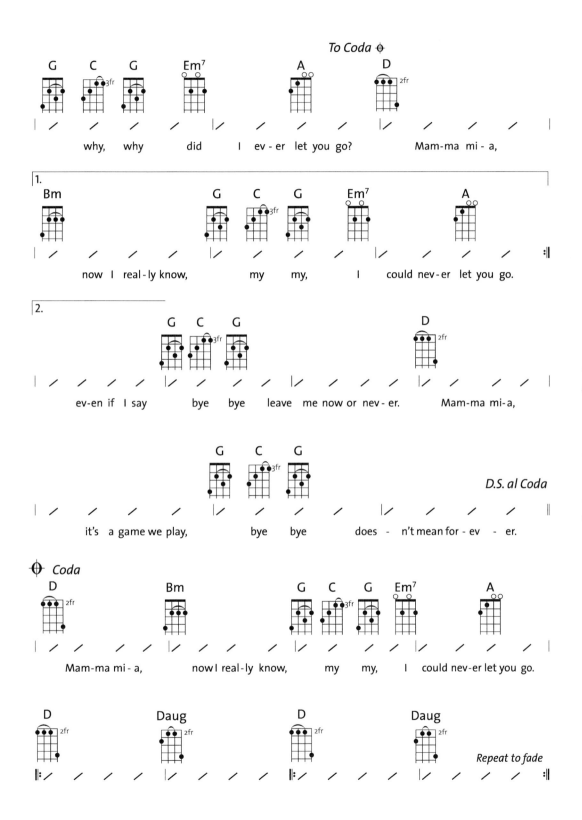

Knowing Me, Knowing You

Words & Music by Benny Andersson, Stig Anderson & Björn Ulvaeus

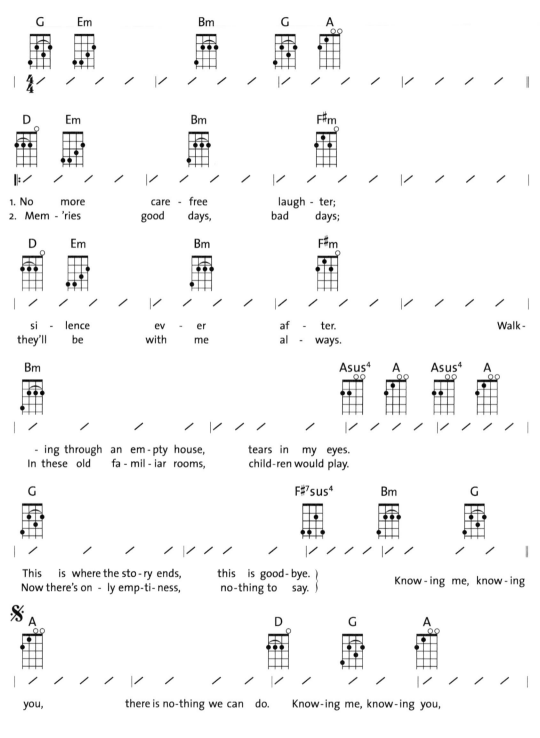

1. No more care - free laugh - ter;
2. Mem - 'ries good days, bad days;

si - lence ev - er af - ter. Walk-
they'll be with me al - ways.

- ing through an em - pty house, tears in my eyes.
In these old fa - mil - iar rooms, child - ren would play.

This is where the sto - ry ends, this is good - bye.)
Now there's on - ly emp - ti - ness, no - thing to say.)

Know - ing me, know - ing

you, there is no - thing we can do. Know - ing me, know - ing you,

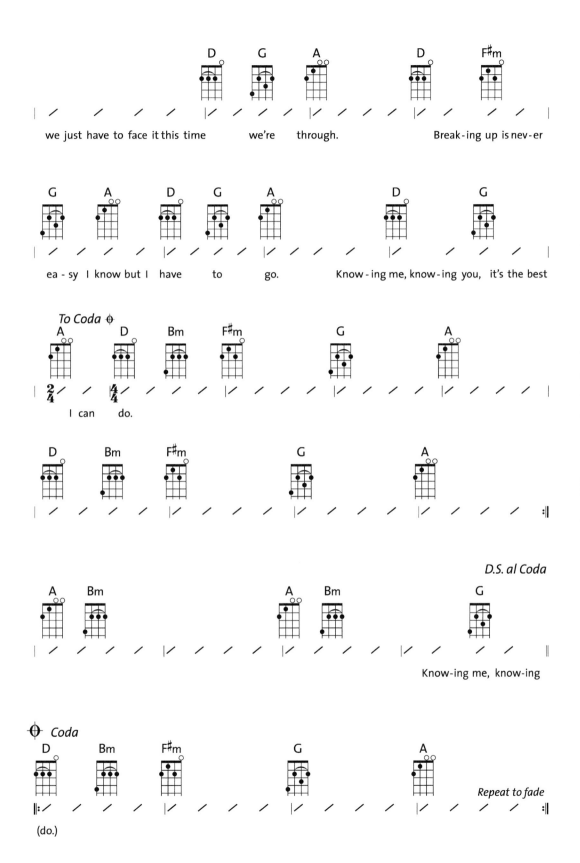

we just have to face it this time   we're   through.   Break-ing up is nev-er

ea - sy I know but I   have   to   go.   Know-ing me, know-ing you, it's the best

To Coda ⊕

I can   do.

D.S. al Coda

Know-ing me, know-ing

⊕ *Coda*

Repeat to fade

(do.)

The Name Of The Game

Words & Music by Benny Andersson, Stig Anderson & Björn Ulvaeus

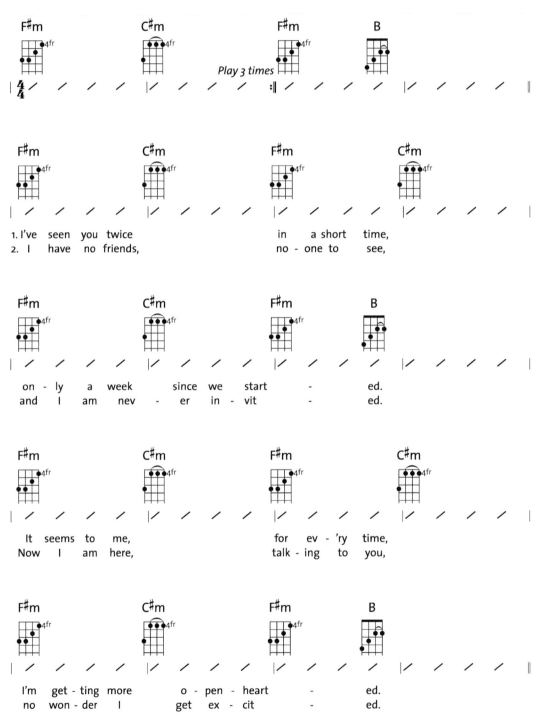

1. I've seen you twice   in a short time,
2. I have no friends,   no - one to see,

on - ly a week since we start - ed.
and I am nev - er in - vit - ed.

It seems to me,   for ev - 'ry time,
Now I am here,   talk - ing to you,

I'm get - ting more o - pen - heart - ed.
no won - der I get ex - cit - ed.

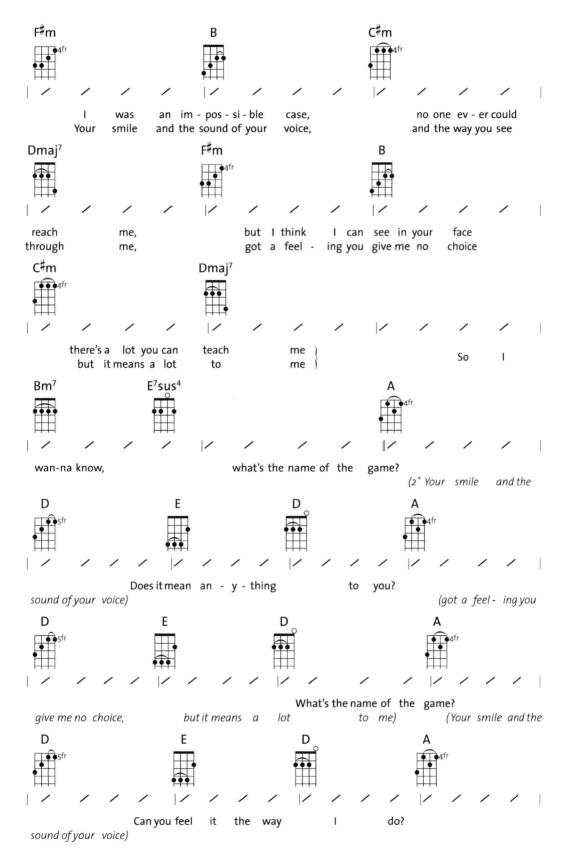

F#m ┃ / / / ┃ B ┃ / / / / ┃ C#m ┃ / / / ┃

I was an im - pos - si - ble case, no one ev - er could
Your smile and the sound of your voice, and the way you see

Dmaj⁷ ┃ / / / / ┃ F#m ┃ / / / / ┃ B ┃ / / / / ┃

reach me, but I think I can see in your face
through me, got a feel - ing you give me no choice

C#m ┃ / / / / ┃ Dmaj⁷ ┃ / / / / ┃ ┃ / / / / ┃

there's a lot you can teach me ⎫ So I
but it means a lot to me ⎭

Bm⁷ ┃ / / / / ┃ E⁷sus⁴ ┃ / / / / ┃ A ‖ / / / / ┃

wan-na know, what's the name of the game?
(2° Your smile and the

D ┃ / / / / ┃ E ┃ / / / / ┃ D ┃ / / / / ┃ A ┃ / / / / ┃

Does it mean an - y - thing to you?
sound of your voice) (got a feel - ing you

D ┃ / / / / ┃ E ┃ / / / / ┃ D ┃ / / / / ┃ A ┃ / / / / ┃

What's the name of the game?
give me no choice, but it means a lot to me) (Your smile and the

D ┃ / / / / ┃ E ┃ / / / / ┃ D ┃ / / / / ┃ A ┃ / / / / ┃

Can you feel it the way I do?
sound of your voice)

23

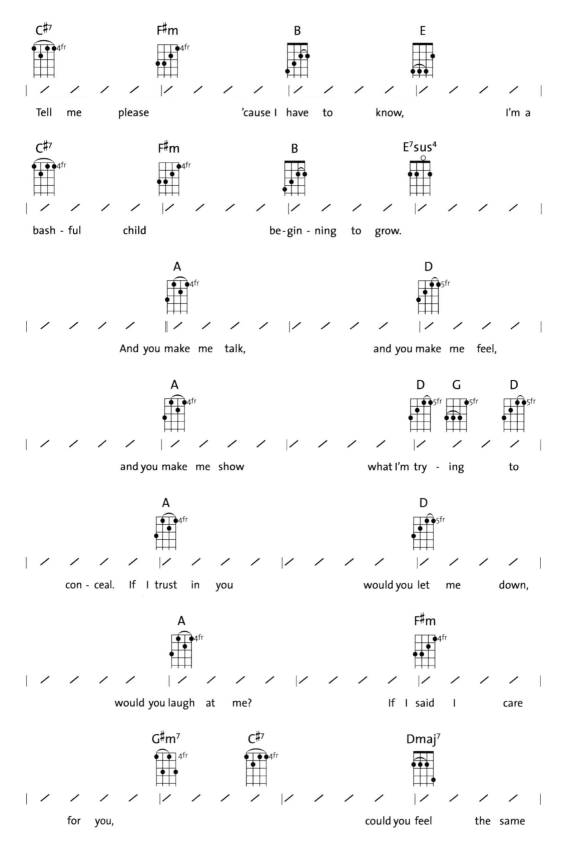

C#7   F#m   B   E

| / / / / | / / / / | / / / / | / / / / |

Tell me please   'cause I have to   know,   I'm a

C#7   F#m   B   E7sus4

| / / / / | / / / / | / / / / | / / / / |

bash - ful child   be-gin - ning to grow.

A   D

| / / / / || / / / / | / / / / | / / / / |

And you make me talk,   and you make me feel,

A   D G D

| / / / / | / / / / | / / / / | / / / / |

and you make me show   what I'm try - ing   to

A   D

| / / / / | / / / / | / / / / | / / / / |

con - ceal. If I trust in you   would you let me down,

A   F#m

| / / / / | / / / / | / / / / | / / / / |

would you laugh at me?   If I said I care

G#m7   C#7   Dmaj7

| / / / / | / / / / | / / / / | / / / / |

for you,   could you feel the same

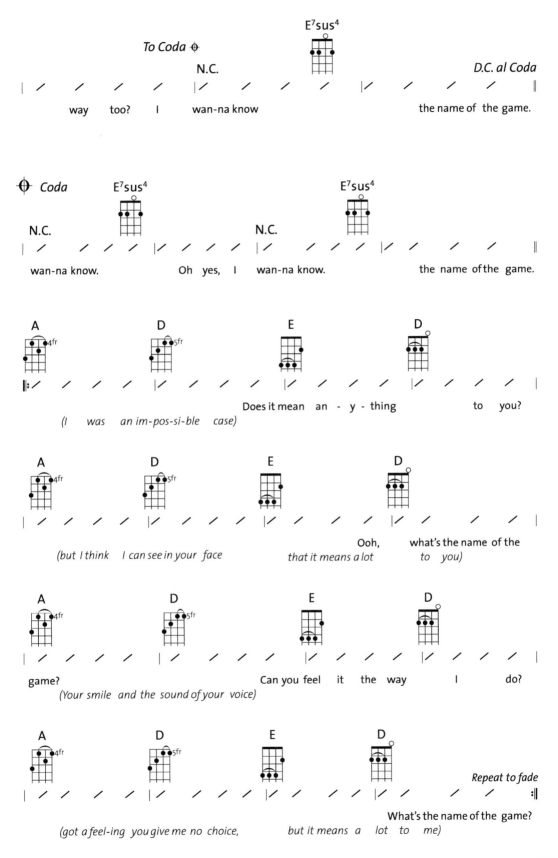

To Coda ⊕

E⁷sus⁴

N.C.

| ✓ ✓ ✓ ✓ | ✓ ✓ ✓ ✓ | ✓ ✓ ✓ ✓ ‖

way   too?   I   wan-na know   the name of the game.

D.C. al Coda

⊕ Coda   E⁷sus⁴   E⁷sus⁴

N.C.   N.C.

| ✓ ✓ ✓ ✓ | ✓ ✓ ✓ ✓ | ✓ ✓ ✓ ✓ | ✓ ✓ ✓ ✓ ‖

wan-na know.   Oh yes, I wan-na know.   the name of the game.

A   D   E   D

‖: ✓ ✓ ✓ ✓ | ✓ ✓ ✓ ✓ | ✓ ✓ ✓ ✓ | ✓ ✓ ✓ ✓ |

Does it mean an - y - thing   to   you?

(I   was   an im-pos-si-ble   case)

A   D   E   D

| ✓ ✓ ✓ ✓ | ✓ ✓ ✓ ✓ | ✓ ✓ ✓ ✓ | ✓ ✓ ✓ ✓ |

Ooh,   what's the name of the

(but I think   I can see in your face   that it means a lot   to   you)

A   D   E   D

| ✓ ✓ ✓ ✓ | ✓ ✓ ✓ ✓ | ✓ ✓ ✓ ✓ | ✓ ✓ ✓ ✓ |

game?   Can you feel   it   the   way   I   do?

(Your smile and the sound of your voice)

A   D   E   D

Repeat to fade

| ✓ ✓ ✓ ✓ | ✓ ✓ ✓ ✓ | ✓ ✓ ✓ ✓ | ✓ ✓ ✓ ✓ :‖

What's the name of the game?

(got a feel-ing you give me no choice,   but it means a   lot to   me)

25

Money, Money, Money

WORDS & MUSIC BY BENNY ANDERSSON & BJÖRN ULVAEUS

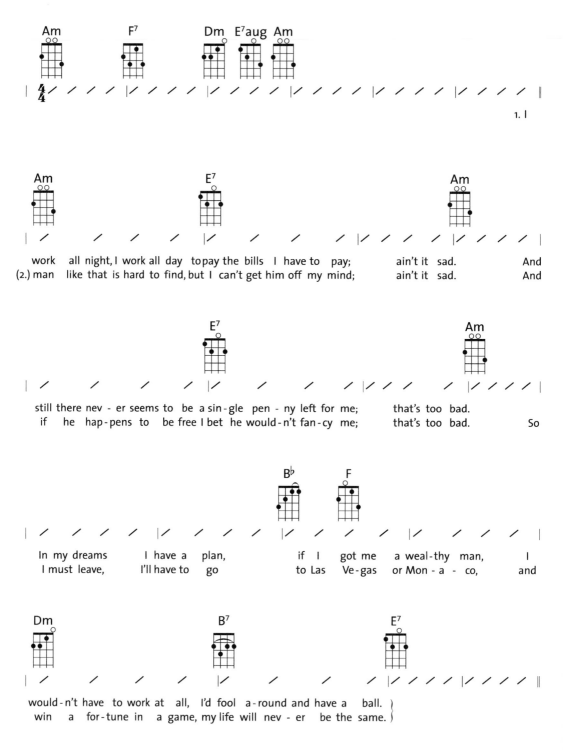

work all night, I work all day to pay the bills I have to pay; ain't it sad. And
(2.) man like that is hard to find, but I can't get him off my mind; ain't it sad. And

still there nev - er seems to be a sin-gle pen - ny left for me; that's too bad. So
if he hap-pens to be free I bet he would-n't fan-cy me; that's too bad. So

In my dreams I have a plan, if I got me a weal-thy man, I
I must leave, I'll have to go to Las Ve-gas or Mon-a-co, and

would-n't have to work at all, I'd fool a-round and have a ball.
win a for-tune in a game, my life will nev-er be the same.

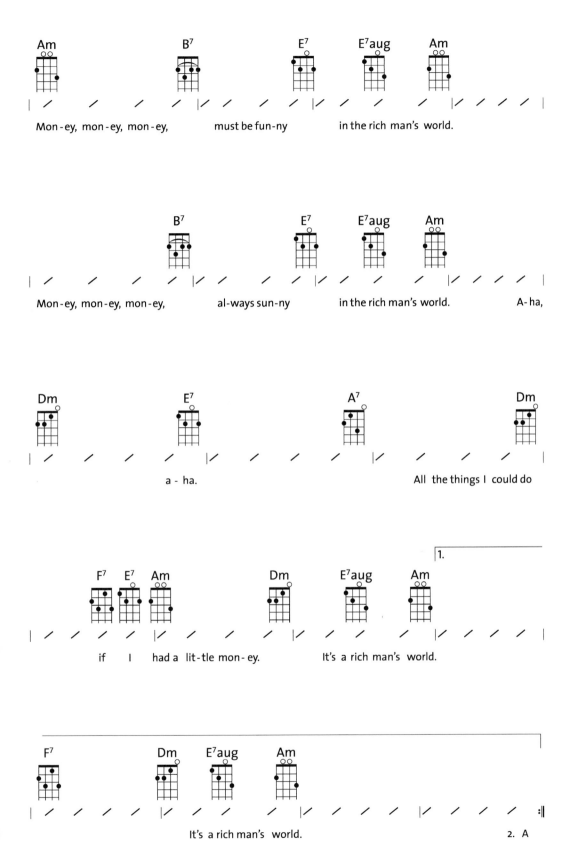

Mon-ey, mon-ey, mon-ey,   must be fun-ny   in the rich man's world.

Mon-ey, mon-ey, mon-ey,   al-ways sun-ny   in the rich man's world.   A-ha,

a - ha.   All the things I could do

if   I   had a lit-tle mon-ey.   It's a rich man's world.

It's a rich man's world.   2. A

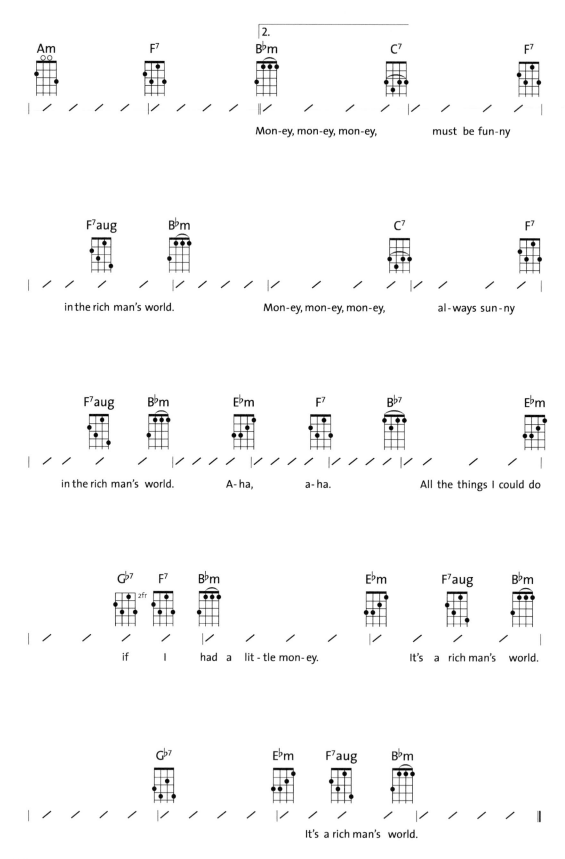

Mon-ey, mon-ey, mon-ey,   must be fun-ny

in the rich man's world.   Mon-ey, mon-ey, mon-ey,   al-ways sun-ny

in the rich man's world.   A-ha,   a-ha.   All the things I could do

if   I   had a lit-tle mon-ey.   It's a rich man's world.

It's a rich man's world.

S.O.S.

WORDS & MUSIC BY BENNY ANDERSSON, STIG ANDERSON & BJÖRN ULVAEUS

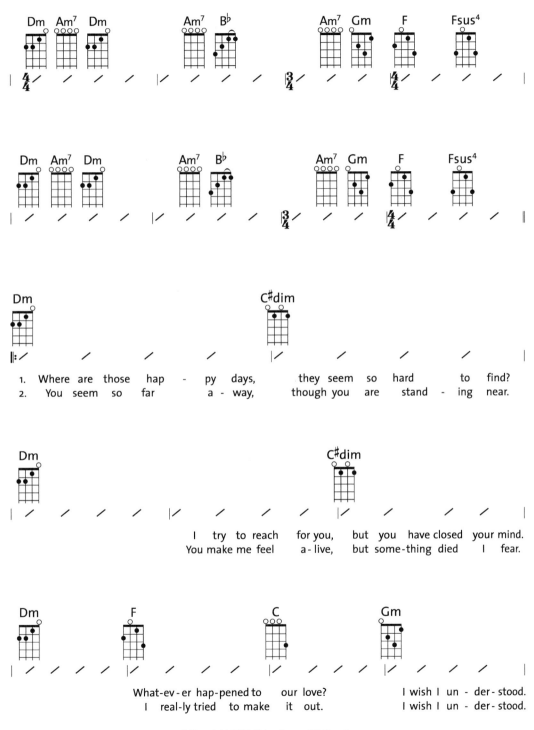

1. Where are those hap - py days, they seem so hard to find?
2. You seem so far a - way, though you are stand - ing near.

      I try to reach for you, but you have closed your mind.
You make me feel a - live, but some-thing died I fear.

What-ev - er hap-pened to our love? I wish I un - der-stood.
I real-ly tried to make it out. I wish I un - der-stood.

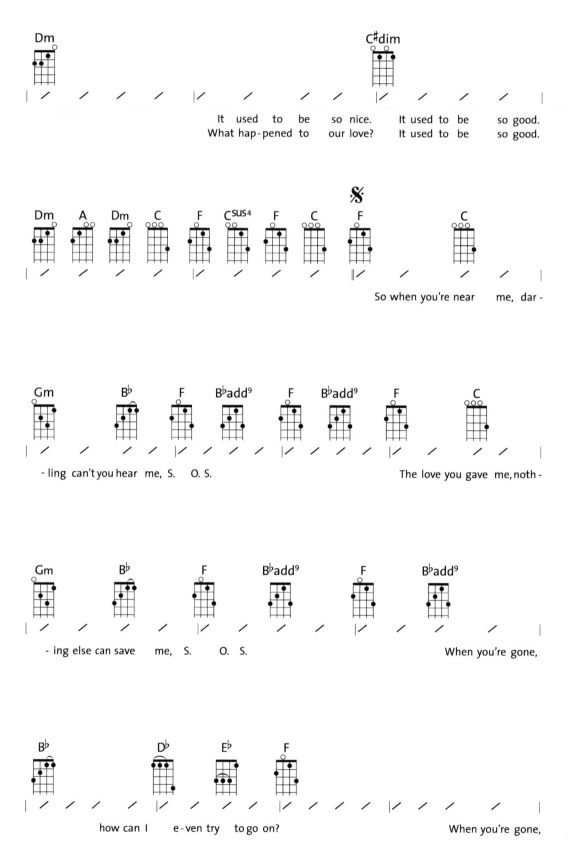

Dm   **C#dim**

It used to be so nice. It used to be so good.
What hap-pened to our love? It used to be so good.

Dm A Dm C F Csus4 F C F C

So when you're near me, dar -

Gm Bb F Bbadd9 F Bbadd9 F C

- ling can't you hear me, S. O. S. The love you gave me, noth -

Gm Bb F Bbadd9 F Bbadd9

- ing else can save me, S. O. S. When you're gone,

Bb Db Eb F

how can I e-ven try to go on? When you're gone,

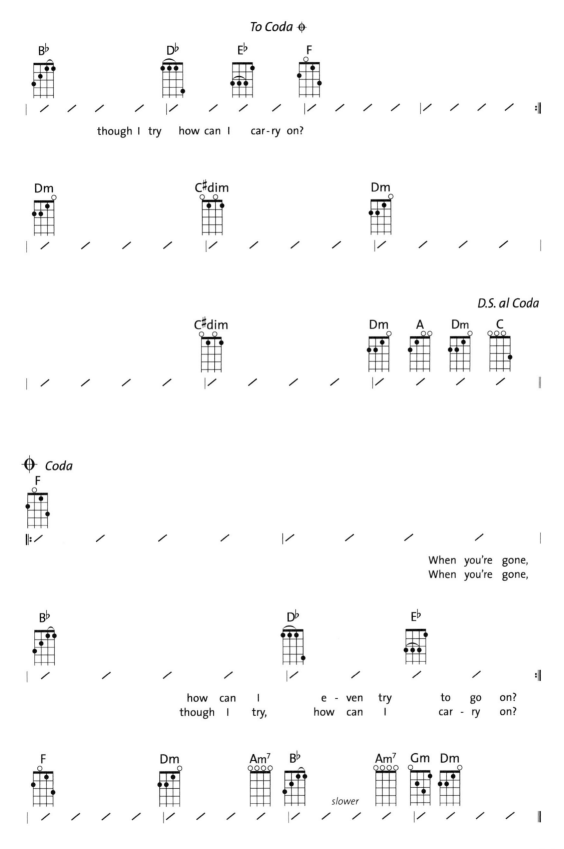

To Coda ⊕

B♭   D♭   E♭   F

though I try   how can I   car-ry on?

Dm   C#dim   Dm

D.S. al Coda

C#dim   Dm   A   Dm   C

⊕ *Coda*

F

When you're gone,
When you're gone,

B♭   D♭   E♭

how can   I   e - ven   try   to   go   on?
though   I   try,   how   can   I   car - ry   on?

F   Dm   Am⁷ B♭   Am⁷ Gm Dm

slower

31

Super Trouper

Words & Music by Benny Andersson & Björn Ulvaeus

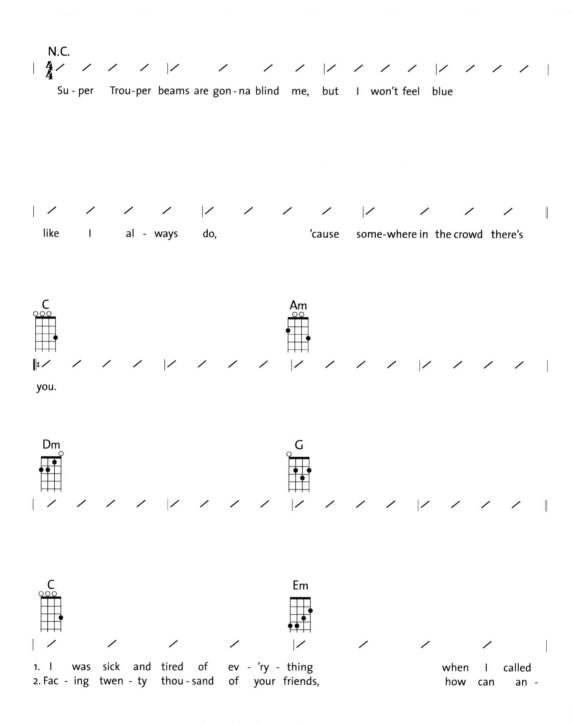

N.C.

Su - per Trou-per beams are gon-na blind me, but I won't feel blue

like I al - ways do, 'cause some-where in the crowd there's

C   Am

you.

Dm   G

C   Em

1. I was sick and tired of ev-'ry-thing when I called
2. Fac-ing twen-ty thou-sand of your friends, how can an -

Dm				G⁶			G	C			

you last   night   from   Glas - gow.   All   I   do   is   eat and sleep and
- y - one   be   so   lone - ly.   Part of a   suc - cess that nev - er

Em			Dm				G⁶		G	F

sing,   wish - ing ev - 'ry show was the last   show.   So   i - ma - gine   I was
ends,   still I'm think - ing a - bout you on - ly.   There are mo - ments when I

C				F			

glad to hear you're com - ing   sud - den - ly   I   feel   all
think I'm go - ing cra - zy,   but   it's   gon - na   be   all

C				F			

right   and   it's   gon - na   be   so
right   ev - 'ry - thing will   be   so

C		Gsus⁴			G		

diff - 'rent when I'm on the stage to - night.)
diff - 'rent when I'm on the stage to - night.)   To - night the

𝄋	C	Csus⁴	C		C	Csus⁴	G

Su - per   Trou - per lights are gon - na find me,   shin - ing like the sun,

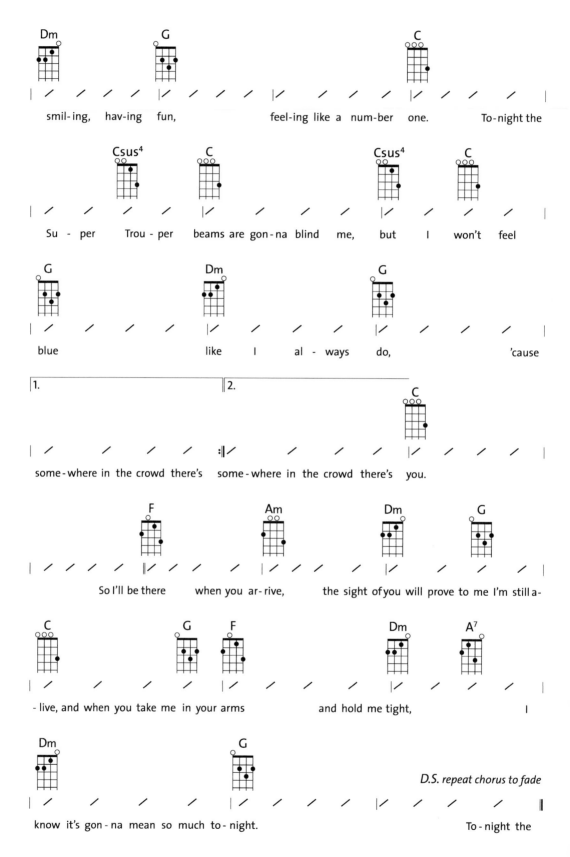

Dm   G   C

smil-ing, hav-ing fun,   feel-ing like a num-ber one.   To-night the

Csus⁴   C   Csus⁴   C

Su - per Trou - per beams are gon-na blind me,   but   I   won't feel

G   Dm   G

blue   like   I al - ways do,   'cause

1.   2.   C

some-where in the crowd there's some-where in the crowd there's you.

F   Am   Dm   G

So I'll be there   when you ar-rive,   the sight of you will prove to me I'm still a-

C   G F   Dm   A⁷

- live, and when you take me in your arms   and hold me tight,   I

Dm   G

D.S. repeat chorus to fade

know it's gon-na mean so much to-night.   To-night the

34

Take A Chance On Me

Words & Music by Benny Andersson & Björn Ulvaeus

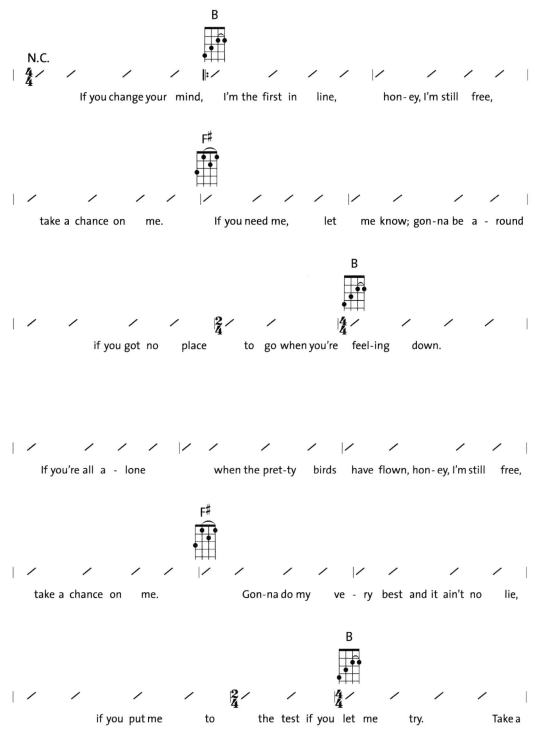

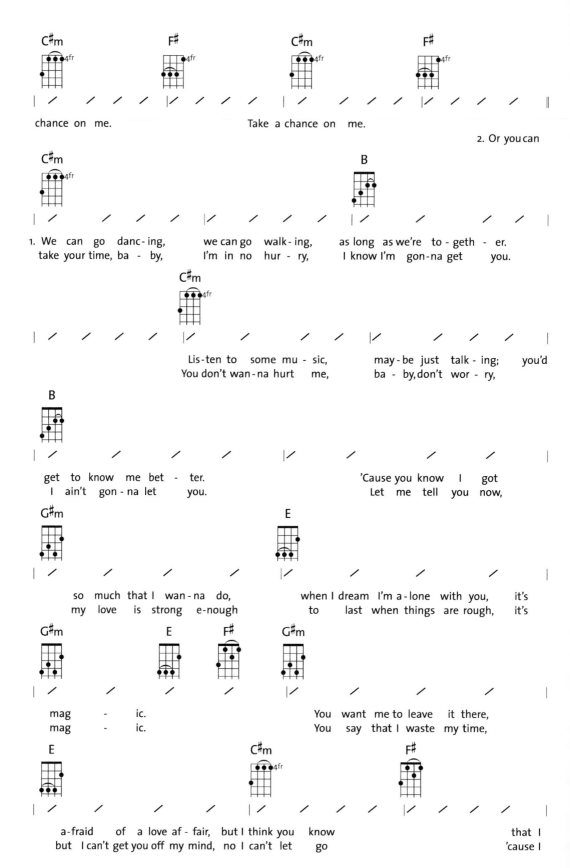

C#m   F#   C#m   F#

chance on me.   Take a chance on me.

2. Or you can

C#m   B

1. We can go danc - ing,   we can go walk - ing,   as long as we're to - geth - er.
take your time, ba - by,   I'm in no hur - ry,   I know I'm gon-na get   you.

C#m

Lis-ten to some mu - sic,   may - be just talk - ing;   you'd
You don't wan-na hurt   me,   ba - by, don't wor - ry,

B

get to know me bet - ter.   'Cause you know   I   got
I ain't gon - na let   you.   Let me tell you now,

G#m   E

so much that I wan-na do,   when I dream I'm a - lone with you,   it's
my love is strong e-nough   to last when things are rough,   it's

G#m   E   F#   G#m

mag - ic.   You want me to leave it there,
mag - ic.   You say that I waste my time,

E   C#m   F#

a-fraid of a love af - fair, but I think you know   that I
but I can't get you off my mind, no I can't let   go   'cause I

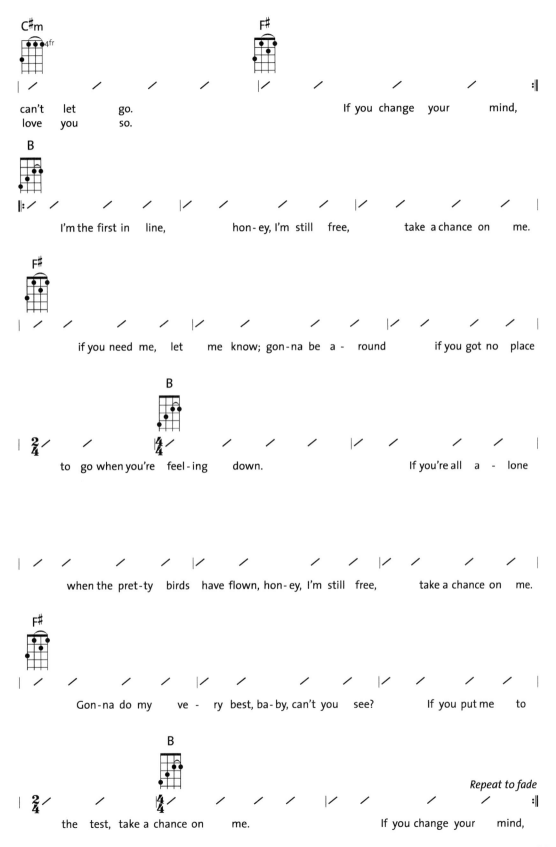

C#m   F#

can't let   go.   If you change   your   mind,
love   you   so.

B

I'm the first in   line,   hon-ey, I'm still   free,   take a chance on   me.

F#

if you need me,   let   me know; gon-na be a - round   if you got no   place

B

2/4   4/4   to go when you're feel-ing   down.   If you're all a - lone

when the pret-ty birds have flown, hon-ey, I'm still   free,   take a chance on   me.

F#

Gon-na do my   ve - ry best, ba-by, can't you   see?   If you put me   to

B

Repeat to fade

2/4   4/4   the   test, take a chance on   me.   If you change your   mind,

37

Thank You For The Music

WORDS & MUSIC BY BENNY ANDERSSON & BJÖRN ULVAEUS

1. I'm no-thing spec - ial, in
2. Moth-er says I was a

fact, I'm a bit of a bore.
dan-cer be-fore I could walk.

If
Mm - mm, she

I tell a joke you've prob-ab-ly heard it be - fore.
says I be-gan to sing long be - fore I could talk.

But I have a tal - ent, a won-der-ful thing, 'cause
And I've of-ten won-dered, how did it all start? Who

ev - 'ry-one lis - tens when I start to sing. I'm so grate-ful and proud,
found out that no - thing can cap-ture a heart like a me - lo-dy can?

all I want is to sing it out loud.)
Well who-ev - er it was I'm a fan.)

So I say:

Thank you for the mu-sic, the songs I'm sing-ing.   Thanks for all   the joy they're bring-ing.

Who can live with-out it? I ask in all hon-est-y.   What would life be?   With-out a song

or a dance, what are we?   So I say, thank you for the mu-sic, for giv-ing it to me.

To Coda ⊕

I've   been so luck-y,   I am the girl   with   gol-den hair.   I wan-na sing

D.S. al Coda

it out   to   ev - 'ry - bo - dy, what a joy,   what a life,   what a chance.

⊕ *Coda*

So I say thank you for the mu-sic, for giv-ing it   to me.

39

Voulez-Vous

WORDS & MUSIC BY BENNY ANDERSSON & BJÖRN ULVAEUS

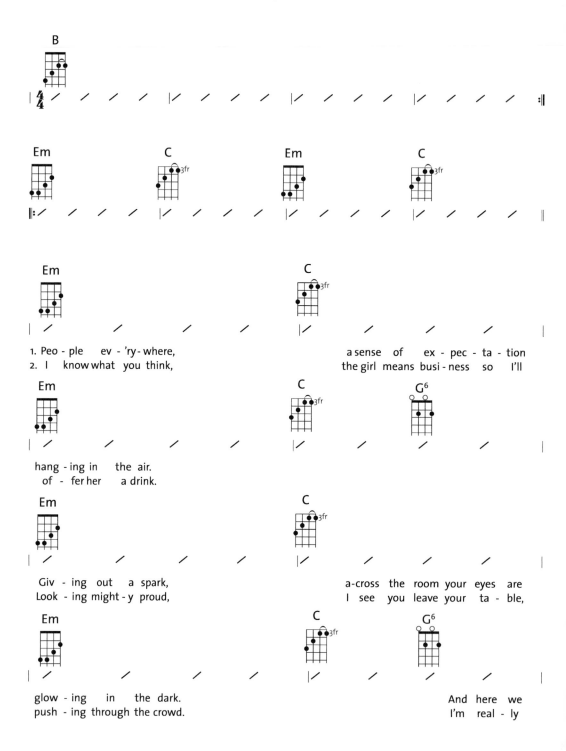

1. Peo - ple ev - 'ry - where,   a sense of ex - pec - ta - tion
2. I   know what you think,   the girl means busi - ness so I'll

hang - ing in   the air.
of - fer her   a drink.

Giv - ing out   a spark,   a - cross the room your eyes are
Look - ing might - y proud,   I see you leave your ta - ble,

glow - ing in   the dark.   And here we
push - ing through the crowd.   I'm real - ly

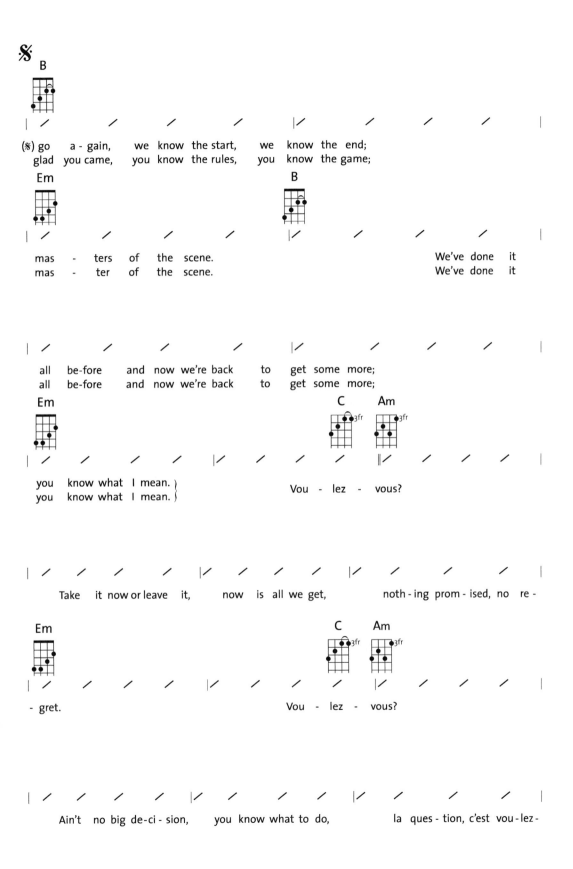

B

| ✓ | ✓ | ✓ | ✓ | | ✓ | ✓ | ✓ | ✓ | |

(%) go a-gain, we know the start, we know the end;
glad you came, you know the rules, you know the game;

Em   **B**

| ✓ | ✓ | ✓ | ✓ | | ✓ | ✓ | ✓ | ✓ | |

mas - ters of the scene.   We've done it
mas - ter of the scene.   We've done it

| ✓ | ✓ | ✓ | ✓ | | ✓ | ✓ | ✓ | ✓ | |

all be-fore and now we're back to get some more;
all be-fore and now we're back to get some more;

Em   **C**   **Am**

| ✓ | ✓ | ✓ | ✓ | | ✓ | ✓ | ✓ | ✓ | | ✓ | ✓ | ✓ | ✓ | |

you know what I mean.)   Vou - lez - vous?
you know what I mean.)

| ✓ | ✓ | ✓ | ✓ | | ✓ | ✓ | ✓ | ✓ | | ✓ | ✓ | ✓ | ✓ | |

Take it now or leave it, now is all we get, noth-ing prom-ised, no re-

Em   **C**   **Am**

| ✓ | ✓ | ✓ | ✓ | | ✓ | ✓ | ✓ | ✓ | | ✓ | ✓ | ✓ | ✓ | |

- gret.   Vou - lez - vous?

| ✓ | ✓ | ✓ | ✓ | | ✓ | ✓ | ✓ | ✓ | | ✓ | ✓ | ✓ | ✓ | |

Ain't no big de-ci - sion, you know what to do, la ques - tion, c'est vou-lez-

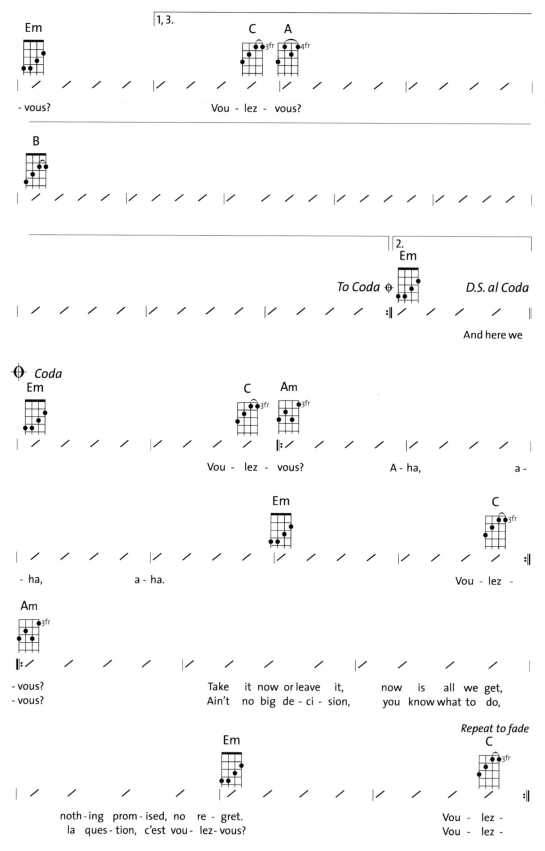

Em |1, 3.| C   A

| / / / / | / / / / | / / / / | / / / / |

- vous?   Vou - lez - vous?

B

| / / / / | / / / / | / / / / | / / / / | / / / / |

                                         |2.
                                         Em
                          To Coda ⊕   D.S. al Coda

| / / / / | / / / / | / / / / |: / / / / |

                                            And here we

⊕ Coda
Em   C   Am

| / / / / | / / / / |: / / / / | / / / / |

     Vou - lez - vous?   A - ha,   a -

                    Em   C

| / / / / | / / / / | / / / / | / / / / :|

- ha,   a - ha.   Vou - lez -

Am

|: / / / / | / / / / | / / / / |

- vous?   Take   it now or leave   it,   now   is   all we get,
- vous?   Ain't   no big de - ci - sion,   you know what to   do,

                                         Repeat to fade
                    Em   C

| / / / / | / / / / | / / / / :|

     noth - ing prom - ised, no re - gret.   Vou - lez -
     la ques - tion, c'est vou - lez - vous?   Vou - lez -

42

Waterloo

WORDS & MUSIC BY BENNY ANDERSSON, STIG ANDERSON & BJÖRN ULVAEUS

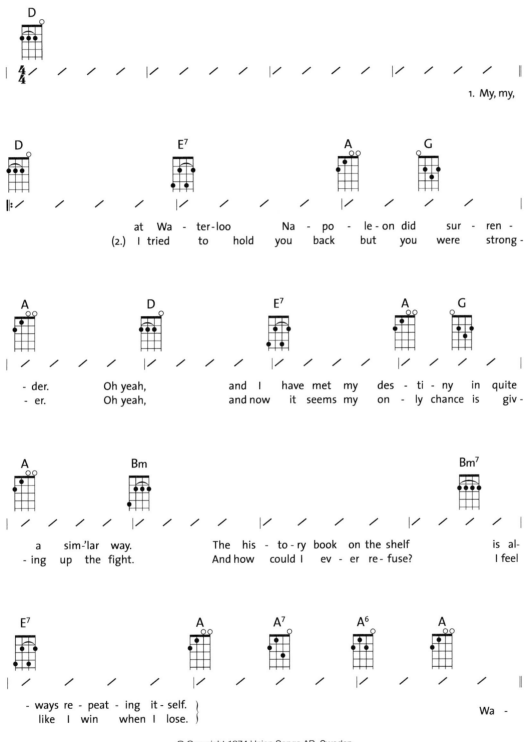

1. My, my,

at Wa - ter-loo   Na - po - le - on did   sur - ren -
(2.) I tried   to   hold   you   back   but   you   were   strong -

- der.   Oh yeah,   and I   have met   my   des - ti - ny   in   quite
- er.   Oh yeah,   and now   it seems my   on - ly   chance is   giv -

a   sim-'lar way.   The   his - to - ry book   on the shelf   is al-
- ing   up the fight.   And how   could I   ev - er re- fuse?   I feel

- ways re - peat - ing it - self.)
like   I   win   when I   lose.)   Wa -

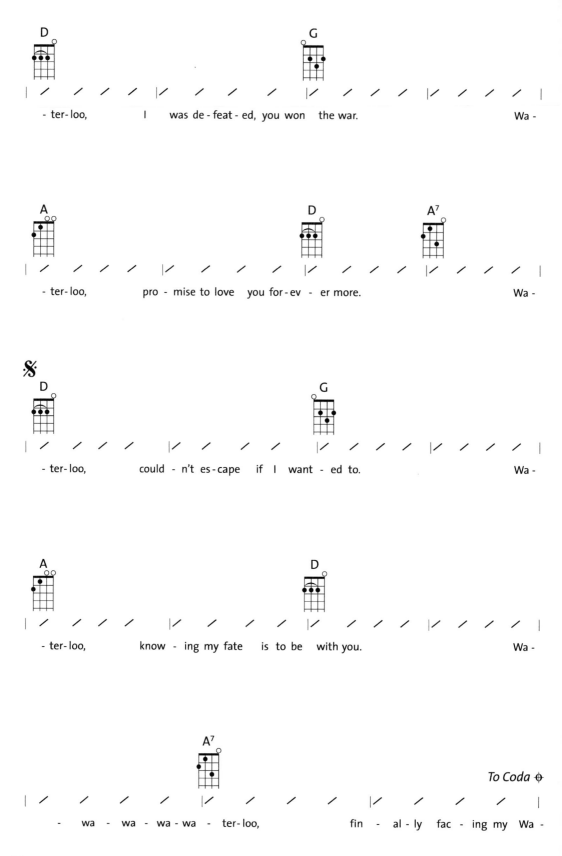

- ter- loo,   I   was de - feat - ed, you won   the war.   Wa -

- ter- loo,   pro - mise to love   you for - ev - er more.   Wa -

- ter- loo,   could - n't es - cape if I want - ed to.   Wa -

- ter- loo,   know - ing my fate   is to be   with you.   Wa -

To Coda

- wa - wa - wa - wa - ter- loo,   fin - al - ly fac - ing my Wa -

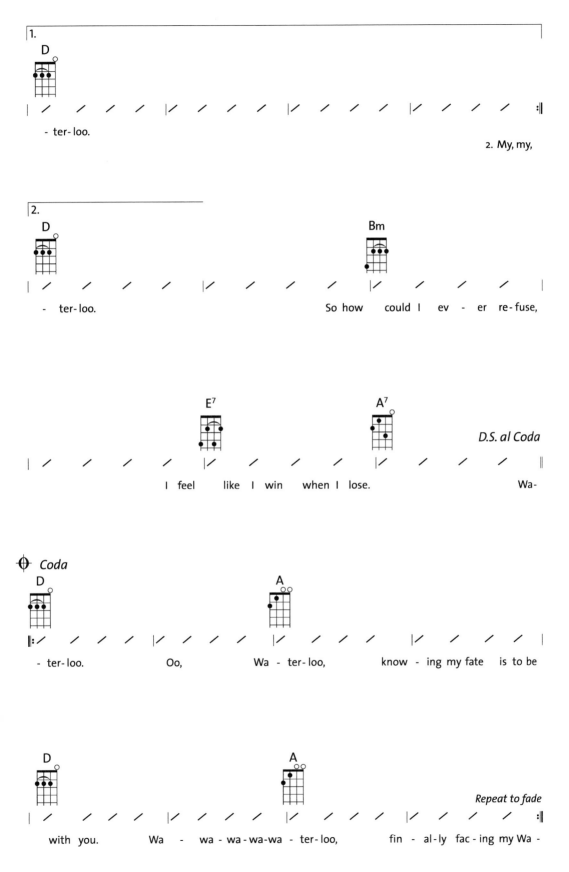

The Winner Takes It All

WORDS & MUSIC BY BENNY ANDERSSON & BJÖRN ULVAEUS

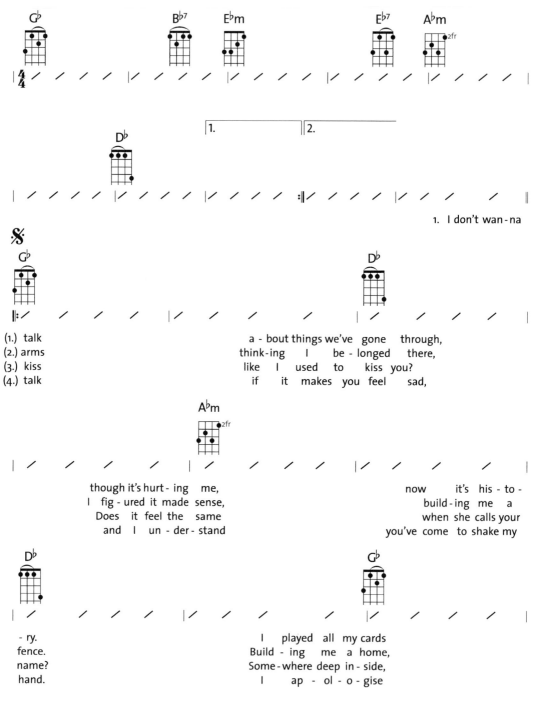

1. I don't wan - na

(1.) talk		a - bout things we've gone through,
(2.) arms		think-ing I be - longed there,
(3.) kiss		like I used to kiss you?
(4.) talk		if it makes you feel sad,

	though it's hurt - ing me,	now it's his - to -
	I fig - ured it made sense,	build - ing me a
	Does it feel the same	when she calls your
	and I un - der - stand	you've come to shake my

- ry.		I played all my cards
fence.		Build - ing me a home,
name?		Some - where deep in - side,
hand.		I ap - ol - o - gise

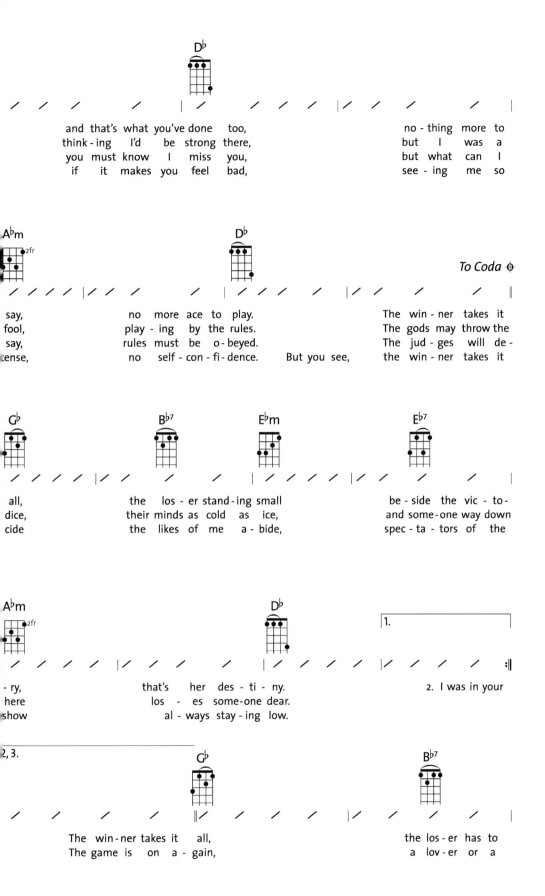

Db

and that's what you've done   too,
think-ing   I'd   be strong there,
you must know   I   miss   you,
if   it   makes you   feel   bad,

no - thing more to
but   I   was   a
but what   can   I
see - ing   me   so

Abm   Db   To Coda ⊕

say,   no   more ace to   play.   The win - ner takes it
fool,   play - ing   by the rules.   The gods may throw the
say,   rules must be o- beyed.   The jud - ges   will de -
tense,   no   self - con - fi - dence.   But you see,   the win - ner takes it

Gb   Bb7   Ebm   Eb7

all,   the   los - er stand-ing small   be - side the vic - to-
dice,   their minds as cold   as   ice,   and some-one way down
cide   the   likes of me   a - bide,   spec - ta - tors of   the

Abm   Db   1.

- ry,   that's   her   des - ti - ny.   2. I was in your
here   los - es some-one dear.
show   al - ways stay - ing low.

2, 3.   Gb   Bb7

The win-ner takes it   all,   the los - er has to
The game is   on a - gain,   a   lov - er or a

47

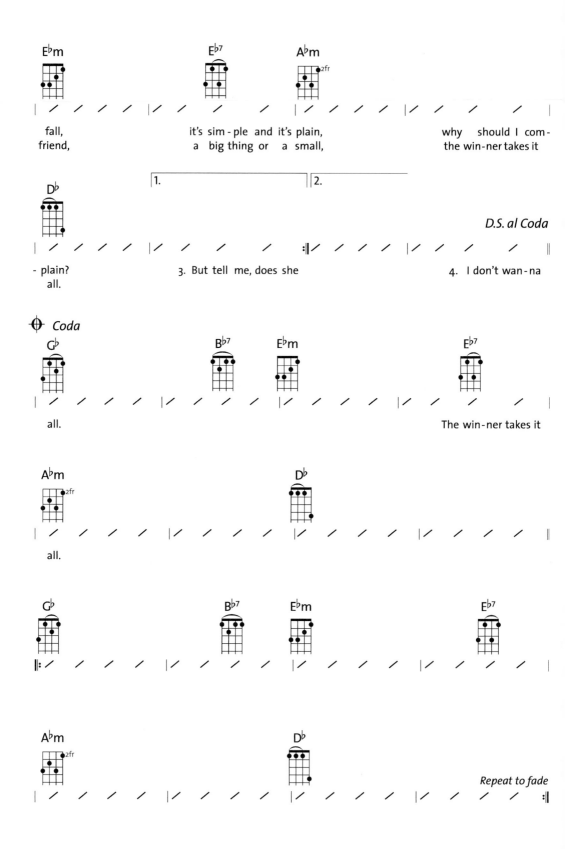

Eᵇm   Eᵇ7   Aᵇm

fall,   it's sim-ple and it's plain,   why   should I com-
friend,   a big thing or a small,   the win-ner takes it

Dᵇ

1.   2.

D.S. al Coda

- plain?   3. But tell me, does she   4. I don't wan-na
all.

⊕ *Coda*

Gᵇ   Bᵇ7   Eᵇm   Eᵇ7

all.   The win-ner takes it

Aᵇm   Dᵇ

all.

Gᵇ   Bᵇ7   Eᵇm   Eᵇ7

Aᵇm   Dᵇ

Repeat to fade